THE
Creative
CANDIDATE

THE
Creative
CANDIDATE

A GUIDE TO COLLEGE ADMISSIONS FOR TEEN ARTISTS

DANA ZULLO

Published by Dana Zullo, www.danazullo.com

ISBN: 979-8-218-73541-8

Cover art by Jason Tan
Back cover art by Lia Lee

Contents

5 Core Lessons on Matching with the Right School

Plus 9 Supplements on How to:

Student Thank-You Notes

"Working with Dana was a great pleasure. She is responsible and offered me a lot of help during my application process. She would email me every other day at important times to check on my progress and made sure I was encouraged to continue. Besides helping me get into a good university, Dana inspired me to grow to become a better individual, and I am very grateful for that." **—Yining Zhang accepted to Washington University in St. Louis (WashU)**

"I want to express my appreciation a thousand times! Thank you for everything, Ms. Dana. I was lucky to have you on this journey with me. Your support helped me not only with my college application, but also in discovering my greatest potential."**—Dlency Zheng, Music Industry and Economics student accepted to University of California Los Angeles (UCLA)**

"Great news! I got accepted to **SAIC with a scholarship!** Your feedback on all the writing helped me a lot. Thank you so much, Ms. Dana!"**—Accepted to School of the Art Institute of Chicago (SAIC)**

"Ms. Dana, **I got into Parsons with a scholarship!** Thank you for your support!"—**Student accepted to Parsons School of Design, The New School**

"Our whole family is so grateful for all the care and support you have given our son! You teamed up with him and gave him incredible support. Your excellent work as well as your guidance, understanding, patience, and all your extra effort helped him and our family survive. We can't thank you enough for being so professional and supportive!"—**Parent of a Neuroscience student and oboe player accepted to University of Southern California (USC)**

"Thank you again for all the support and help along my application journey. I feel very blessed to have had you as my counselor, Ms. Dana. You always stayed calm and positive even during the most challenging parts of the process, which was really important as sometimes I was feeling very stressed. You always had my best interests at heart, and constantly encouraged me and guided me every step of the way, from picking majors to editing essays. I appreciate all your efforts that went into my application, and it feels amazing to share this exciting news with you! I don't think I would have been able to achieve this without you. My parents and I truly thank you for everything you did for me."—***Ethnomusicology student and classical pianist accepted to Cornell University***

"Thank you so much for your encouragement regarding our daughter's Creative Resume and Video Supplement for UChicago.

We are impressed by the resume she has accomplished. Your summary provides us with a clear picture of her achievements. Your praise of our daughter's work ethic and potential is heartwarming. As parents, it's reassuring to hear such positive feedback from an experienced professional like yourself.

"We are thankful for the individualized attention you're providing to her, including possible short films to present as a creative supplement to UChicago, movie and director recommendations that fit with her interests, and further research on the Columbia Digital Humanities Center. These are all invaluable components of this process.

We fully support your approach and trust your expertise. We are comforted knowing that our daughter is in such capable hands during this crucial time."—**Parent of a film student candidate at University of Chicago**

"Hi Dana, I wanted thank you for your help with my creative resume and portfolio. Your advice truly made a difference in how I presented my work! Your encouragement and guidance have meant a lot to me! I'm excited to continue growing and learning, and I'll definitely keep you updated on my progress." —**Iris Boyun, Film student accepted to University of Southern California (USC)**

"Dear Dana, I'm truly grateful I had the chance to work with you throughout my application process. It was such a privilege and I really enjoyed every moment. The artistic resume we created together undoubtedly strengthened my NYU application, and I can't thank you enough for all your support and guidance." —**Sophie Li, Dance student accepted to New York University (NYU)**

For all the creative teens—

Your skills and ideas matter. Keep creating, keep exploring—you will make the world a better place.

Foreword

Dear Creative Candidate,

It's an honor to share my journey with you—a story that began with a vulnerable but ultimately rewarding decision to submit my art portfolio when I applied early to Columbia Engineering over 25 years ago. Back then, it was a paper application, and I remember slipping my art into the envelope, wondering: *Am I good enough?* That question lingers in the hearts of many creative students, and I'm here to say—unequivocally—*Yes, you are.*

I didn't fully realize it at the time, but submitting that portfolio helped me claim my identity as both an artist and an engineer. I was admitted, and when I arrived on campus, I visited the School of the Arts. Professor Gregory Amenoff looked at me and said, "I've seen this before." My undergraduate portfolio had crossed his desk—something normally reserved for MFA candidates. That moment affirmed that creativity and engineering aren't opposites. They are kin.

I'm a third-generation oil painter and engineer, raised in the Hindu Vedic tradition in Edison, New Jersey. After witnessing 9/11 as a Columbia student, I wrote *The Vital*

Breath, a yoga-political romance, and began a lifelong devotion to hatha yoga. I live by a simple mantra: *The longer the breath, the calmer the mind.*

Over the years, my paintings have traveled far—*Kathak Dancers* received a New York Times review and was acquired by the Rubin Museum. Then, something surreal happened: it was selected for the Lunarprise Mission. Along with three other works—including *Mars Meditation*, created while I chanted Sanskrit under my 3D-printed space helmet—my art was etched onto quartz disks and launched on a Falcon 9 rocket to the Moon's south pole.

So yes, I submitted an art portfolio to an engineering school—and eventually, my art landed on the Moon.

To every young artist-engineer-dreamer flipping through these pages: trust your instincts, follow your breath, and let your brush reach for the stars. You never know where your truth might take you.

Veru Narula

Foreword

Times Square, New York, NY: *Climate Refugees*

"If I can make it there, I'll make it anywhere..."
— Frank Sinatra

Artwork courtesy of Jean Kwak accepted to Chelsea College of Art, University of the Arts London

Title: Astro Bunny
Medium: Acrylic paint
Year: 2022

Foreword

Artwork courtesy of Yuki Sun, accepted to Sarah Lawrence College majoring in Film Directing and Playwriting

Title: The Sun
Medium: Digital art in Sketchbook
Year: 2021

Artwork courtesy of Amy Pan, accepted to the Dual Degree Program at Brown University majoring in Science, Technology and Society and Rhode Island School of Design (RISD) majoring in Graphic Design

Title: Seafoam Sparkle
Medium: Recycled fabric, yarn, and beads
Year: 2024

Welcome!

I am here to inspire and guide young creatives like yourself as you pursue a fulfilling path in the arts. I am a college counselor, published writer, and experienced arts professional. I have a background in galleries, museums, and higher education. I have the experience to support you in navigating your art school applications.

I want to help you grow and showcase your talents with confidence—whether through exploring creative flow, writing compelling essays, or finding your ideal college fit.

Let's lift your creative life to new heights!

Artwork courtesy of Shayna Shapiro, with a major in Advertising and Marketing Communications accepted to the Fashion Institute of Technology (FIT)

Untitled
Medium: Eyeshadow palette
Year: 2020

Introduction for the Teen Artist

Dear Teen Artist,

This guide is designed to help you navigate the college admissions process and create a standout art and design portfolio that reflects your unique voice. As you embark on this exciting process, remember that your portfolio is more than a collection of work—it is a glimpse into who you are, featuring your interests, ideas, and the creativity you will bring to campus.

Throughout these pages, you will find core lessons on crafting a clear, compelling portfolio that comes alive off the page, showcases your talents, and stands out to admissions readers. Whether you are a painter, designer, musician, performer, or filmmaker, this guide will show you how to highlight the technical skills, creativity, and storytelling ability that set you apart. When you apply the lessons you learn here, I am confident you will be successful at your right-fit college.

Wishing you much success in both your creative and academic endeavors. The world needs more people like you—individuals who bring self-expression, collaboration, communication, attention to detail, and imagination into everything they do. Keep creating and let your talent shine!

To forever learning and creating,

Dana Z.

Artwork courtesy of Amy Pan, accepted to the Dual Degree Program at Brown University majoring in Science, Technology and Society and Rhode Island School of Design (RISD) majoring in Graphic Design

Title: Transformation
Medium: Acrylic paint on canvas
Year: 2024

Artwork courtesy of Lia Lee, accepted to Hongik University in Korea majoring in Fashion Design

Title: The two of you
Medium: Acrylic paint
Year: 2021

quiet studio,
echoes of dreams and triumphs,
your art finds its voice.

CHAPTER *1*

Discover Your Creative Self

As you stand on the brink of a new chapter in your life, the path to college becomes about more than just higher education; it is a chance to delve deep into who you are as an artist and as an individual. This chapter is about understanding yourself and reflecting on the accomplishments that have shaped your unique creative development.

Finding Your Creative Space

Picture yourself in a quiet space, perhaps a studio filled with the remnants of your artistic endeavors—sketches, films, musical scores, or design prototypes. This is your personal haven, where the echoes of your creativity are most vibrant. Here, amidst the clutter of past projects and half-finished ideas, is where you will start to uncover the essence of your artistic self.

Begin by simply being present in this space. How? Let your surroundings "speak" to you. This is where you have poured your ideas, hopes, and energy into your craft. In this reflective space, you will begin to tap into a deeper understanding of your identity as an artist.

Introspection—Exploring the Highlights

Now, begin the process of introspection. Ask yourself: *What moments in my creative life have filled me with happiness and purpose?* Was it the exhilarating feeling of completing a challenging piece, or the satisfaction of seeing your work come to life on screen, stage, or canvas? Reflect on those moments, for they are the cornerstones of your artistic identity.

Think of that one project that ignited your interest or the first time you saw your ideas blossom into reality. These snapshots are not only highlights—they are glimpses into your true artistic self. These are the times you've felt the spark that propels you forward.

Overcoming Challenges— Acknowledge Your Growth

Next, think about the hurdles you have faced and conquered. Each obstacle you have overcome—whether mastering a difficult technique, navigating a creative block, or pushing through self-doubt—has sculpted you into the artist you are today. These experiences are not just struggles; they are milestones that highlight your resilience and growth.

Challenges have a way of sharpening our focus and revealing our strengths. What are the struggles you've overcome, and how have they shaped your creative voice? Reflecting on these will deepen your understanding of your own tenacity and commitment to your craft.

Documenting Your Process— Creating a Portfolio or Journal

Creating a portfolio or journal is a powerful tool in articulating your individual identity. Document your creative process, your projects, and the feedback you've received. This archive will not only track your evolution but will also reveal patterns in your work and highlight the progress you've made. It is a tangible representation of your narrative filled with the lessons you've learned and the artistic milestones you've achieved.

A well-documented creative history will also become an invaluable resource as you prepare for college. It shows a cohesive narrative of your growth, dedication, and vision. Whether in written reflections or a collection of works in your chosen media, this documentation is proof of your artistic identity.

Seeking Insight—Engaging with Mentors and Peers

Seek out conversations with mentors, teachers, or fellow artists, and ask them how they view your work and your artistic style. Their perspectives will offer new insights into your strengths and areas for growth. Often, these people see what you might overlook in your own work, providing valuable feedback and illuminating the special aspects of your distinctive voice.

Your mentors and peers have not only witnessed your progress, but they are also valuable mirrors, reflecting back parts of your work and talent that you may not fully appreciate. Through these dialogues, you will gain new insight on where your clever strengths lie.

Celebrating Your Individuality

As you reflect, remember to celebrate your individuality. Your path is uniquely yours, shaped by your experiences, interests, and vision. When you look back on your accomplishments, take a moment to consider how they contribute to your distinctive artistic identity.

No two storylines are the same. What makes your work special is the personal touch you bring to every project. As a teen, you may sometimes want to fit in more than you want to stand out, emulate rather than innovate. That's understandable. But, I encourage you to celebrate your uniqueness and recognize it as a strength that will guide you through the next steps of your education and beyond.

Embracing the Process

This process of self-discovery and reflection is not just about preparing for college; it's about understanding and embracing who you are as a creator. Sometimes you'll be surprised by what you find during this process; let these words from a student guide you in recognizing the value of your progress and the promise of your future endeavors:

"My message to students currently in the application season is this: everything that happens is ultimately beneficial for you, and it's never too late to make a change based on your inner desires.

When I first started the college application process, I wasn't clear about my future direction. Interestingly, it seems like most important life events are compressed into the ages of 18 to 30. In this short span of time, we are expected to figure out our passion, complete our education, find a job that is considered excellent by societal standards, and even find a life partner.

However, in reality, life offers far more opportunities for trial and error than we imagine, and we can leave ourselves some space for exploration.

Because of my strong interest in painting, I initially discussed applying to art schools with my application advisor, Ms. Dana. But during the preparation process, I realized that pursuing advanced studies in art didn't excite me, and I couldn't imagine myself working in the art industry. I love art but don't want my passion for it to turn into my job or become constrained by external pressures; rather, I wanted art to remain very personal to me.

When the pandemic hit, I discovered a deep interest in international politics. The different pandemic policies of various countries sparked my curiosity about their national contexts. Within a week, I studied the modern history of six countries and came to understand the logic behind their pandemic policies.

At this point, my application process was already halfway through, and starting over would have been a significant challenge. Fortunately, with Ms. Dana's support, I successfully shifted my focus to applying to universities with strong international relations programs. Ultimately, I was admitted to George Washington University's Elliott School of International Affairs.

Looking back now, I know that decision was absolutely right because I maintained great enthusiasm for this field throughout my four years at university and achieved many accomplishments.

Currently, I am applying for graduate studies in international relations to continue advancing in this field. At the same time, I've been exploring ways to combine politics, history, and art, creating works that would have been impossible without prior intellectual accumulation.

During college, I also met many peers who hadn't decided on their majors as freshmen. Although they were seen as 'late bloomers,' their extensive exploration often helped them identify a direction they truly loved and allowed them to pursue their chosen paths with depth and verve.

Applying to college is not as decisive as it is exploratory; if you're going through this process, don't put too much pressure on yourself. And remember, it's never too late to make a change."—**Jane, accepted to George Washington University majoring in International Affairs**

Next, you'll start researching schools, but before you get to that step, complete the reflection process by embracing your creative self. Celebrate your achievements, honor your growth, and look forward with excitement to the new artistic horizons that lie ahead.

"You can't use up creativity. The more you use, the more you have."—**Maya Angelou**

Creativity grows with practice. The more you sketch, write, design, or play, the more ideas will come. Don't worry about "saving" inspiration—let it flow and trust that more will follow.

Action Steps: Showcase Your Creative Development

- Take a photo of something that reminds you of why you started creating. Keep it as a visual reminder on your phone.
- Unearth an object or piece of art from your childhood that inspired you—keep it on your desk as a reminder of your growth.
- Swap a piece of art with a friend or classmate. See what you can learn from each other's styles or approaches. When you swap back, you will see your creation with fresh eyes.

JOURNAL PROMPTS:
Discover Your Creative Self

Take time to reflect on these questions. Is there one that resonates with you the most? Answer directly in this book or open a page on your computer or phone. Jot down dot points or respond in free-flowing sentences or verse. Your answers will be useful in your college application essays or college interviews.

1) Think about the progression that led you to this point as an artist. What was the first spark that ignited your creativity?

2) Describe a moment when you felt truly connected to your art and what it revealed about you. Reflect on how this experience has shaped your character as a creative.

3) What values or themes are emerging in your work, and why do they matter to you?

Artwork courtesy of Juhi Kundu, accepted to Princeton University majoring in Mechanical Engineering

Title: Butterfly Brain
Material: Digital Art in Procreate
Year: 2024

Artwork courtesy of Juhi Kundu, accepted to
Princeton University majoring in Mechanical
Engineering

Title: Diwali Lantern
Medium: Cardboard lantern
Year: 2024

dreams find their true home,
campus hums with art and light,
vision shapes the path.

CHAPTER *2*

Find Your Creative College Fit

For creative students who want to make their career in art, design, or any form of artistic expression, applying to college is about more than just picking a school—it is about finding a place that inspires you, challenges you, and helps you grow as an artist. Here is how you can research a range of colleges, explore their academic programs, and find the social atmosphere that is right for you.

Start with Self-Reflection

Before diving into college research, think about what you want from your college experience. Do you see yourself at a bustling urban campus surrounded by galleries and cultural institutions, or do you prefer a quieter, more intimate setting where you can focus on your craft? Knowing what kind of environment you thrive in will help you narrow down your options.

My student, Yining Zhang, had this to say about her story of getting accepted at Washington University in St. Louis (WashU):

"First, adopt the mindset of being competent and deserving of the schools' acceptance. Talking to friends and family who support and understand you is also very important because they know you well and can see your strengths, which you might have a tendency of overlooking about yourself.

Second, remember that a school's most important assets are the people in it, and by being accepted at a certain school, you are helping to build its community and culture. Knowing this, you can see how *you* are the one that makes the school better, not the other way around."

Keep Yining's wisdom in mind as you move on to the next step!

Research Colleges with Reputable Art and Design Programs

Look for schools that have an excellent reputation in your area of interest, whether that is fine arts, graphic design, fashion, animation, or any other creative field. Start by exploring specialized art schools—like Rhode Island School of Design (RISD), Savannah College of Art and Design (SCAD), Art Center College of Design (ACCD), Parsons School of Design, The New School, School of Visual Arts (SVA), or the Pratt Institute—which offer intensive programs focused entirely on creative disciplines. Also, consider larger universities with renowned art departments that can provide a mix of creative and traditional academic experiences, like Boston University, Chapman University, Syracuse University, or University of California Los Angeles (UCLA).

Explore Academic Programs and Curriculums

Once you have a list of potential schools, dive deeper into their academic offerings. First, peruse the courses to see if they match your interests. Do they have strong foundational courses, leading-edge technology, or innovative approaches to art and design? Next, review their faculty—are they active professionals in your industry? Finally, check out the schools' website or social media pages to view student work and exhibitions, which will give you an idea of the kind of work that is encouraged and produced.

Consider the Campus Facilities

For artists and designers, facilities matter. Among the colleges you researched, look for the ones with the studios, labs, and technology you need to bring your ideas to life. Do they have digital labs, printmaking studios, 3D printers, or other equipment that is important for your work? Many schools offer virtual or on-campus tours where you can see these spaces firsthand. Having access to top-notch facilities will make a difference in your creative development.

Understand the School's Social Atmosphere

College isn't just about the academics—it is also about the community. You'll want to find a place where you feel comfortable and inspired, especially if you'll be living on campus. Research the school's social environment by looking at student organizations, clubs, and co-curricular activities related to the arts. Are there student-run galleries, design clubs, or opportunities to collaborate on creative projects? Understanding the school's culture will help you find a place where you can connect with like-minded peers.

Look into Internship and Career Opportunities

As a creative, gaining real-world experience is crucial. Research how each college supports its students in finding internships, residencies, or industry connections. Some schools have strong ties to the creative industry and offer robust career services that can help you land internships at design firms, art galleries, or tech companies. Knowing that a college actively supports your professional growth will make a big difference in your artistic development post-college.

Attend College Fairs, Virtual Info Sessions, and Portfolio Days

Take advantage of opportunities to interact with schools directly before you start the application process. College fairs, virtual information sessions, and National Portfolio Days are golden opportunities to meet admissions representatives, ask questions, and get a feel for the schools you are interested in. These events can also give you insights into what each college is looking for in its applicants.

Trust Your Instincts

Finally, remember that choosing a college is a personal decision, made with your family's support. Trust your instincts about what feels right for you. If a campus visit or a conversation with a professor leaves you excited and inspired—or not—pay attention to that feeling. Your college years are a time to explore, create, and grow, so find the place that feels like home for your creative progress.

Choosing the right college is a big decision, but by exploring your options thoroughly and considering what matters most to you, you'll find a school that is the right match for your artistic ambitions. Embrace the process, and get ready to discover a community that celebrates your creativity!

"Success is liking yourself, liking what you do, and liking how you do it."—Maya Angelou

Success is about growing into the kind of artist (and person) you're proud to be. Colleges know that, and acceptance letters will come.

Action Steps: Match Your Goals with the School's Offerings

- Watch a video walkthrough or take a virtual tour of a college that interests you. Pay attention to anything that excites you, and see if it sparks new ideas for your own work.
- Take a few minutes to silently observe something you would like to create. Pay attention to its textures, shapes, and colors as if you are capturing it with your mind.
- Find one image that represents your ideal school (e.g., their colors, their logo, or a photo of campus). Keep it as a background on your phone or laptop for motivation.

Journal Prompts: Connecting with Colleges and Programs

Take time to reflect on these questions. Is there one that resonates with you the most? Answer directly in this book or open a page on your computer or phone. Jot down dot points or respond in free-flowing sentences or verse. Your answers will be useful in your college application essays or college interviews. (When we work together I have a spreadsheet you can use for college research.)

1) Research at least 10 colleges or programs that interest you. For each, write down specific aspects— such as courses, professors, or opportunities—that excite you.

1.
2.
3.
4.
5.
6.
7.
8.
9.
10.

2) Imagine yourself on campus: what would your ideal day look like?

3) How do you envision contributing to that school's community, and what do you hope to gain in return?

Artwork courtesy of Amy Shi, accepted to Rice University majoring in Biosciences

Title: Temporal Trifecta
Medium: Oil Paint and Acrylic
Year: 2024

Artwork courtesy of Valentine Liu accepted to The New School, Parsons School of Design

Title: Drawing practice
Medium: Drawing needle pen on paper
Year: 2023

words shape who you are,
sketches, drafts, stories refined,
vision flows like art.

CHAPTER 3

Create and Refine Your Application and Essays

A
pplying to college as a creative student means you have an opportunity to leverage your talents, voice, and artistic vision in your application and essays. Your application is more than just a list of grades and activities—it is a reflection of who you are as an artist. Here's how to design and refine your application and essays to ensure they represent the best version of you and attract the attention of college admissions staff.

Showcase Your Distinctive Progress

Your application and essays are your chance to tell your story. Admissions committees want to understand you as an artist or innovator—how you got started, what drives your artistic expression, and where you want to take your craft next. Using your work from Chapter 1, think about key moments that shaped your individual growth, such as a project that challenged you, a piece that reflects your perspective, or a personal experience that influenced your special path. Use these moments to highlight your growth, determination, and artistic vision in your application.

Develop a Compelling Personal Narrative

Your essay is the perfect place to let your personality shine. Rather than trying to impress with fancy language or a list of accomplishments, focus on writing from the heart. Share your creative process, what inspires you, or a particular art field you're interested in. Be specific—describe a moment when you felt truly connected to your work, the late nights spent perfecting a piece, or the thrill of seeing your film on screen for the first time. These personal touches make your story memorable and will resonate with the people with the power to send you an acceptance letter.

Highlight Your Process

Colleges are interested in not just what you create, but how you create it. In your essays and supplemental materials, talk about your process. Do you start with sketches and thumbnails, dive straight into editing film, or collect inspiration from everyday life? Do you thrive on collaborating with others, or do you find solace in working solo? Describing your process will give admissions officers insight into your approach to problem-solving, innovating, and artistic thinking.

Match Your Goals with the School's Offerings

When writing essays, especially "Why this college?" prompts, research the specific resources, programs, or professors that excite you. Mention how you are drawn to their state-of-the-art studios, renowned faculty, unique course offerings, or the school's vibrant creative community. Demonstrating that you've done your homework shows that you are genuinely interested in what the school has to offer and how it matches with your artistic goals. Tell how studying at this college will help get you where you want to go in the future.

Show, Don't Just Tell

As a creative, you have the advantage of using vivid language and imagery to paint a picture with your words. Instead of simply stating that you're passionate about filmmaking, describe a scene: the hum of your camera as you capture the ideal shot, the way you lose track of time editing late into the night, or the moment you see your vision come to life on screen. Use your storytelling skills to make your essays come alive, just as you would with your art.

Revise, Edit, and Seek Feedback

Creating a standout application isn't about getting it perfect on the first try—it's about refining your work, just like you would with an art piece or film edit. Write multiple drafts of your essays and give yourself time to revise. Seek feedback from trusted teachers, mentors, or peers who understand your creative voice. Their edits and recommendations will give you insights on clarity, tone, and whether your story comes across the way you intend. Every edit brings you closer to your best work, so don't be afraid to make changes—but also know when it's time to stop tweaking and just press "Submit"!

Improve Your Artist Statement

If your application requires an artist statement, use it to explain your artistic vision, your influences, and the themes that run through your work. Be genuine and specific. Rather than saying you love to create, delve into why you create. What messages are you trying to convey? What impact do you hope your work will have? A detailed artist statement gives context to your portfolio, helps admissions understand your voice, and distinguishes your application from the many others they are reviewing.

Curate a Cohesive Portfolio

For creative students, your portfolio is as important as your written application. Select pieces that best represent your skills, interests, and range. Include works that showcase your growth and are most reflective of your style and vision. If you're a filmmaker, make sure your reel highlights a variety of techniques. If you are a designer, include projects that demonstrate your problem-solving skills and aesthetic.

You get the idea—each piece should tell a part of your story and form a larger, cohesive narrative about who you are as an artist.

Embrace Your Natural Voice

Throughout the application process, stay true to who you are. Don't try to fit into a mold or create an image of what you think colleges want to see. Your authenticity, purpose, and character are what set you apart. Let your perspective shine through in every aspect of your application.

Here is what two students had to say about the importance of finding the right school for you while staying true to your artistic vision:

"As an artistic student, fit is more important, and you shouldn't get caught up in the race to the top if it isn't right for you."—**Neuroscience major and oboe player at University of Southern California (USC)**

"Trust that where you end up will be the best fit for you. I reminded myself of this even in the face of unsuccessful early rounds—and it turned out to be true. This is without a doubt one of the most stressful times you'll experience, but I wouldn't have it any other way. The college application process is an opportunity to reflect on your journey and learn how to share your story with someone who's never met you. As you condense your colorful and complex life into what might seem like a mere

10-item activity list, think of it as a chance to decide what to leave behind and what to carry forward into college. Success lies in showing what you truly love and are passionate about."—**Dlency Zheng, University of California Los Angeles (UCLA) B.A. Music Industry and Economics**

Crafting a compelling application is your chance to let colleges see the artist behind the work. With thoughtful storytelling, careful curation, and a genuine reflection of your progress, you will design an application that truly captures your distinctive spirit.

"The progression of an artist is a continual self-discovery."—Georgia O'Keeffe

Your portfolio doesn't have to be perfect—but let it show who you're becoming. Let it evolve, be honest, and be full of discovery.

Action Steps: Highlight Your Creative Process

- Document your process by taking a few short videos or photos during different stages of your next project. Capture your setup and materials, the messy work in progress, and the polished final piece.
- Make a small "mood board" using magazine clippings, items from nature, or anything that represents your

current creative catalysts. If you prefer, you can also go digital with free tools such as Pinterest, Pexels or a collage app like Layout. Keep your mood board near your workspace for inspiration.

• Ask a friend to describe your art in three words. Use their language to reflect on how others see your work and what you want to express through it.

Journal Prompts: Creating and Refining Your Application and Essays

Take time to reflect on these questions. Is there one that resonates with you the most? Answer directly in this book or open a page on your computer or phone. Jot down dot points or respond in free-flowing sentences or verse. Your answers will be useful in your college application essays or college interviews.

1) Reflect on what makes your story unique. What are the core values and motivations that drive you and your work?

2) Think about a challenging or pivotal moment in your artistic narrative. What did you learn, and how has it influenced your art?

3) In what ways do you see your voice influencing your artistic choices and your goals for the future? What do you like making and why?

Artwork courtesy of Evan Sun, accepted to Emory University majoring in Quantitative Biology and Business

Title: Emulation of Boy with a Basket of Fruit by Caravaggio
Medium: Photography
Year: 2022

Artwork courtesy of Yang Liu, accepted to Rhode Island
School of Design (RISD) majoring in Illustration

Title: Frozen Ocean
Medium: Oil on canvas
Year: 2025

pieces fall in place,
stories of art softly told,
true self on display.

CHAPTER

Organize Your Creative Supplements

Applying to college as a creative student often means going beyond the standard application. In addition to your essays and transcripts, you will likely be asked to submit supplemental materials such as a portfolio, music repertoire, or creative resume. These components showcase your talent and interests, so it is essential to organize and present them in the best possible way.

Putting everything together can feel like a lot to juggle at once, but you can set yourself up for success, and reading this book is the first step! And if you are feeling the pressure, remind yourself that you are looking for your right fit, as my students say:

> "Applying for college is tough—you have to balance practicing your craft, preparing the pre-screening, writing personal statements, and completing schoolwork. I was fortunate to have Ms. Dana's help during this process. She freed up my time by guiding

me through brainstorming for my personal statement and by providing professional advice. If I could offer advice to my younger self, I would tell myself not to stress too much. Being able to present a 'realer' self to the schools is more important than worrying about how to look better on paper. What *will* impress the admissions office are genuine, heartfelt expressions in both your music performance and essays."—**Taylor Yi, Classical Saxophone student at Vanderbilt University**

"Always maintain focus and self-confidence in yourself, love what you are doing at the moment, and do not worry about tomorrow. Managing time wisely is also key, and remember to break each goal into smaller objectives and tackle them step by step until you succeed. Lastly, failure is not something to fear; learning from the experience is vital to growth."— **Jason Tan, Illustration and Entertainment Design student at Art Center College of Design (ACCD)**

Here is how to make a strong impression with your creative supplements:

Understand the Requirements

Each college will have specific guidelines for submitting creative supplements, so start by carefully reading the instructions for each school. Some may have specific requirements on the number of pieces, formats, or mediums, while others offer more flexibility. Knowing what is expected will help you tailor your submission to meet their criteria and avoid missing any key elements.

Curate Your Best Work

Whether you are putting together an art portfolio, a music repertoire, or a performance video, quality matters more than quantity. Select works that showcase your strengths, versatility, and distinctive style. Choose pieces that you feel most proud of and that represent your creative process. For visual artists, this might mean including a mix of drawings, paintings, and digital work. For musicians, consider including solo performances, ensemble work, and pieces that highlight your technical skill and emotional expression.

Create a Cohesive Narrative

Think of your supplemental items as telling a story about who you are as a creative. Arrange your portfolio so that each piece flows into the next, highlighting your growth. For example, you might start with foundational pieces that show off your technical skills, followed by more experimental or complex works that demonstrate your problem-solving abilities. Musicians and performers can order their pieces to showcase a range of styles and emotions, moving from classical to contemporary or from a soft ballad to an up-tempo composition.

Improve Your Creative Resume

Unlike a traditional resume, a creative resume features your artistic achievements, performances, exhibitions, workshops, and any relevant skills. (If you shudder at the thought of staring at a blank page, Canva is a free online tool with hundreds of templates you can choose from as a starting point.) I also have many examples from real students to share with you when we work together! List your experiences in reverse chronological order, starting with the most recent. Highlight key accomplishments, such as awards, gallery shows, performances, or notable collaborations. Be sure to include relevant details like dates, locations, and roles you played in each project. Your resume should encapsulate the breadth and depth of your body of work, showing your commitment to your craft.

Pay Attention to Presentation

Presentation matters, especially for visual artists and performers. Ensure your portfolio is clean, organized, and visually appealing. When uploading physical art, make high-quality scans of your work or take photographs of it with good lighting and minimal distractions. For digital submissions, label your files clearly and consistently, and according to guidelines provided by the school. Musicians and filmmakers should ensure audio and video recordings are clear and well-edited, and showcase your performance at its best.

Write Clear and Insightful Descriptions

Many colleges will ask for brief statements about each piece you include in your portfolio. Use this space to provide context, explain your process, or share what inspired the work. For a painting, you might discuss the themes you explored or the techniques you used. Musicians can include information about the composer, the significance of the piece, and what it means to you as a performer. Keep descriptions concise, providing insight without overwhelming the reader. They are reading applications very fast and looking for interesting insights!

Seek Feedback and Refine

Before submitting your supplements, get feedback from trusted mentors, teachers, or professionals in your field. They will provide valuable insights on the strength of your selections, the order of your pieces, and the overall presentation. Refining your submission based on their expert feedback shows your commitment to excellence, and your supplementals will be all the better for it. I love advising on the selection and organization of the portfolio. Some students come to me with 20-30 pieces because they need advice knowing what to present and what works well together. These discussions in our meetings are always exciting and filled with energy!

Test Your Digital Submissions

When submitting materials online, make sure all files open correctly, play smoothly, and meet the technical requirements of each college's application system. Test your links, check your file names and sizes, and ensure that everything looks and sounds as intended. This final step requires an exacting focus and attention to detail, but do not skip it—you will prevent technical glitches that might otherwise have undermined your hard work.

Be True to Your Voice and Vision

Above all, ensure that your supplemental items reflect who you are as an artist, musician, or performer. Do not try to mold your work to fit what you think admissions committees want to see. Instead, focus on presenting your genuine creative voice. Your enthusiasm, originality, and dedication to your craft will shine through when you stay true to yourself.

The right creative supplements will greatly enhance your college application, making a powerful statement about your talent and potential. Approach this process with care, creativity, and confidence, and your work will speak for itself.

"I am seeking. I am striving. I am in it with all my heart."—Vincent van Gogh

This is the energy that makes a portfolio come alive. You do not need to have it all figured out—show that you care deeply about your art.

Action Steps: Curate a Cohesive Portfolio

- Choose one small detail in a project you are working on to improve or change. It could be color, texture, or even a small finishing touch.
- Take photos of three of your favorite pieces. Arrange them in different orders on your computer or phone to see which sequence best tells your story.
- Hold a "mini gallery" in your room. Put up a few of your best pieces and step back to see how they look together. Notice if any do not fit the theme.

Journal Prompts: Building Your Portfolio

Take time to reflect on these questions. Is there one that resonates with you the most? Answer directly in this book or open a page on your computer or phone. Jot down dot points or respond in free-flowing sentences or verse. Your answers will be useful in your college application essays or college interviews.

1) Look at the pieces in your portfolio and consider why you chose them. What do they reveal about your growth, your interests, and your skills?

2) Identify one piece that feels especially meaningful to you and explore why it stands out.

3) How does your portfolio as a whole represent your unique vision? How do you hope admissions officers will interpret your body of work?

Artwork courtesy of Shayan Ali, accepted to University of California San Diego (UCSD) majoring in Cognitive Science with a Design specialization

Title: smile!
Medium: Colored pencils on blue paper
Year: 2024

Artwork courtesy of Jason Tan, accepted to Art Center College of Design (ACCD) majoring in Illustration for Entertainment Design

Title: Hat-trick
Medium: Procreate digital art
Year: 2022

future lights the path,
canvas wide, dreams paint the sky,
bold steps, stars align.

CHAPTER 5

Look Ahead to Your Bright and Creative Future

As you prepare to take the next big step towards your future, it's clear that your story is just beginning. You have already spent years exploring your interests, honing your skills, and expressing yourself through art, music, design, film, or whatever your chosen creative outlet. Now, as you apply to college, you are not just looking at a degree—you are paving the way for a vibrant, interesting life full of possibilities. Here is how to keep looking ahead with confidence and excitement as you step into this new chapter.

Embrace the Unknown and Be Open to Growth

One of the most exciting parts of being a creative student is that your future is not set in stone—it is a blank canvas waiting for you to fill it! College will introduce you to new techniques, perspectives, and opportunities you may never have imagined. Be open to exploring new mediums, taking classes outside your comfort zone, or collaborating with peers from different disciplines. Whether you are studying animation, music composition, or fine arts, the willingness to experiment and evolve will be an asset.

Find Inspiration Everywhere

As you look toward your college years, remember that inspiration is all around you. Your future campus will be filled with potential muses, like the architecture and energy of the environment, conversations with classmates who share your interests, or late-night brainstorming sessions in the studio. Keep your eyes and heart open to the world around you. Often, the best ideas come when you are not even looking for them—while people-watching in a park, listening to a new genre of music, or exploring a new city street.

Set Big Goals, but Enjoy the Process

It is important to have dreams—winning an award, exhibiting in a gallery, producing a short film, or performing on a big stage—but remember that your creative process is just as important as the destination. The ups and downs, the failed experiments, and the breakthroughs are all part of what makes your work special. Set ambitious goals for your future, but do not forget to celebrate the small victories along the way. Every sketch, song, or scene is a step forward.

"Flowers may bloom again, but a person never has the chance to be young again." -Chinese Proverb

Build Your Artistic Network

College will be teeming with fellow creatives—people who will not only become friends but also your future collaborators, mentors, and supporters. Take advantage of the vast network available to you: join clubs, participate in student exhibitions, and engage with the local creative community. Your network can lead to future projects, jobs, and partnerships that will help shape your career, so build (and nurture) new relationships at every opportunity.

Stay True to Yourself

As you grow and learn, remember that your artistic voice is what sets you apart. It is easy to get caught up in trends or compare yourself to others, but the world doesn't need another copy of someone else—it needs your perspective, your ideas, and your vision. Stay true to what makes your work genuine, do not be afraid to take creative risks, and resist the pull of the artistic rut. The most memorable artists, designers, and creators are those who dare to be different.

Embrace Challenges as Opportunities

The path of a creative is rarely a straight line. You will face challenges, from creative blocks to tough critiques, but each obstacle is an opportunity to learn and grow. Use setbacks as a chance to reflect, rework, and refine your approach. Resilience is a key trait of every successful artist, and learning to navigate challenges now will prepare you for a rewarding career in your industry.

I love the wisdom in this student's words for anyone facing obstacles in their college application process:

"To future fellow artists: If you find yourself lost, uncertain, or struggling with the process, don't worry—you already have a vision, and with time, you will move closer toward your dreams."

Sincerely, A Fellow Traveler
—**Lily Gui, film student at Boston University**

Dream Big and Keep Creating

The world is full of opportunities for creatives—whether you are dreaming of opening your own design studio, composing soundtracks for films, designing art that moves people, or anything in between. Your future is bright because of your talent and drive. So keep dreaming big, stay inquisitive, and keep creating.

On the path to college and beyond, embrace the twists and turns, stay curious, and let your interests guide you. Your future is waiting, and it is going to be extraordinary. Keep your head up, your heart open, and your creativity flowing—amazing things lie ahead!

"I play the notes as they are written, but it is God who makes the music."—**Johann Sebastian Bach**

Trust that when you put in the effort, something bigger flows through you. Your job is to stay open and committed.

Action Steps: Embrace Your Natural Voice

- Spend a day wearing an accessory or piece of clothing that represents your personality, like a funky hat, bold scarf, or colorful socks. How did it make you feel? How did you react?
- Pick a quote from a favorite artist or creator that resonates with you, and put it somewhere you will see often. Let it be a reminder of your purpose and interests.
- Listen to music that you feel reflects your style as an artist. Let it inspire you to stay true to your message and vision no matter what the day may bring.

Journal Prompts: Staying Resilient and Embracing the Process

Take time to reflect on these questions. Is there one that resonates with you the most? Answer directly in this book or open a page on your computer or phone. Jot down dot points or respond in free-flowing sentences or verse. Your answers will be useful in your college application essays or college interviews.

1) What keeps you motivated even when the path is uncertain?

2) Think about your future as an artist—how do you see yourself contributing to your school, family, community, state, nation, the world?

3) What message do you want your art to have? What do you want the viewer to "take-away" from your art?

Message for the Teen Artist

Dear Teen Artist,

I believe in your creativity and am impressed by your talent. You have important work to do—work that only you can bring into the world. You have a story inside you that needs to be told, and it will resonate with and change others in ways you never thought possible. Your ideas, talents, and contributions are inspiring. Your message and your art matter.

Even when you question your place or feel uncertain, keep going. College is the perfect time for learning, growing, and discovering who you are as an artist and a human being. It is a chance to experience everything, to learn as much as you can, to fall and rise back up, and to connect with peers and professors who will guide you along the way.

You and your art offer something special to the world. I believe in you. I know you have the talent, creativity, and excitement to match with the college that will support your art and career goals. Continue practicing, developing, and documenting your work. As creatives, we thrive on this— it is what fuels us. We do not need to fit into a traditional 9-to-5 job, and that is okay. Our direction may be winding, but along the path, we pick up gems of inspiration.

I wrote this guide for any teen artist, performer, designer, filmmaker, musician, dancer, or creative soul who wants to develop a portfolio that truly represents their gifts and matches them with a school where they will succeed. If you would like to work with me personally as your college counselor and art adviser, reach out directly via email at zullodana@gmail.com, visit my website www.danazullo. com, or connect with me on LinkedIn where I share art and college information.

I am excited to help you present your best self through your application and portfolio. Opportunity is waiting for you!

To forever learning and creating,

Dana Z.

Artwork courtesy of Lia Lee, accepted to Hongik University in Korea majoring in Fashion Design

Title: In the making
Medium: Acrylic paints
Year: 2021

Tips for Aspiring Artists Applying to College

1. **Be Yourself**: Show who *you* are through your work. Do not try to make art you think colleges want to see—make the art that feels true to you.
2. **Tell a Story**: Whether it is your portfolio, essays, or interviews, connect your art to your personal story and why it matters to you.
3. **Quality Over Quantity**: Include fewer pieces if needed but make sure every piece is strong and intentional.
4. **Experiment**: Show versatility—colleges love seeing how you think and adapt.
5. **Stay Open to Feedback**: Critiques are part of the process. Use them to grow, try not to take it personally (a challenge, I know!)
6. **Show Your Process**: Colleges like seeing a few examples from sketchbooks, drafts, or unfinished ideas—it proves you are thoughtful and invested in your growth.
7. **Manage Your Time**: Deadlines come faster than you think. Stay organized, plan ahead, and do not leave submissions to the last minute. Have a guide like a parent, teacher, (or me!) to help you.
8. **Trust Your Voice**: No one sees the world exactly the way you do. That is your edge—use it.
9. **Have Fun**: Keep the joy of creating in your heart. It is what brought you here in the first place.

Artwork courtesy of Yuki Sun, accepted to Sarah Lawrence
College majoring in Film Directing & Playwriting

Title: Caiwei
Material: Digital Art
Year: 2020

Artwork courtesy of Lia Lee, accepted to Hongik University in Korea majoring in Fashion Design

Title: Winter
Medium: Acrylic paint and collage
Year: 2021

Supplemental 1: A Short Guide to Preparing an Art Portfolio for College

"This is your exhibit of work: Curate a selection of pieces that speak to you. Consider experimentation and personal making. Less is more."—**The New School, Parsons School of Design**

"Show what inspires you! We like to see developed concepts and evocative ideas, not just technical exercises."—**Rhode Island School of Design (RISD)**

Requirements

For traditional schools: The creative portfolio is optional and does not need to be major-specific. It can include paintings, drawings, prints, sculptures, ceramics, etc.

For some art schools: You will need to review the specific requirements by major. For instance, photography, film, architecture, and production design each have their own requirements.

"We look for flexible, curious, and critical makers."
—**University of California Los Angeles (UCLA)**

What to Include

Include about 15 examples of your most recent work (from high school and especially the last two years) that showcases your thinking and making, in any medium, finished or sketch form.

The majority should feature finished pieces, with some research or preparatory work in about three portfolio selections.

Include 3–5 examples that involve drawing from direct observation. Examples of observational works include landscapes, still-lifes, self-portraits, figure drawings, and interior spaces.

> "A portfolio is a collection of your work, which shows how your skills and ideas have developed over a period of time. It demonstrates your creativity, personality, abilities and commitment, and helps us to evaluate your potential."—**University of the Arts, London (UAL)**

What to Leave Out

Do not put excessive visual elements and text descriptions together in a single slide. There is a separate box in Slideroom (a third-party website where you have to make an account in order to upload your portfolio for the college) to write the description.

Do not include copies of famous artworks, or work that replicates anime drawings, cartoons, or video game character designs.

Tips

- Additional detail shots can be uploaded as a video or composite.
- Watch portfolio webinars (offered for free by art colleges) and examples from students on YouTube.
- Get your portfolio reviewed for free at National Portfolio Day.
- Please reach out to me for advice! I love to help students on their portfolio presentations, artist statements, written descriptions for portfolio pieces, and art school interview preparation.

Guidelines

1) This is your opportunity to communicate your technical skills and inspire your audience.
2) Provide your best works. Showcase a variety of tools, techniques, processes, and art forms. Include process/development work if permitted
3) Be bold. Choose works that best communicate your goals and aspirations. Highlight your skills and goals to align with those of the college. If you are not sure what they are, read the school's motto, vision statement, and values.

4) Include some personal, independent, self-directed work that you completed outside the classroom. This gives admissions committees an indication of your current involvement and interest in the arts.

5) As you apply to various institutions, tailor your portfolio to each college. Visit admission pages on art school websites to ensure your portfolio meets all the necessary requirements.

Portfolio Checklist

- Is your work personal?
- How are you displaying your process?
- Are you using space effectively?
- Are you exploring different forms of media?
- Have you documented your work properly?
- Do your inclusions tell a cohesive story?

For Multi-Media Artists: Advice from Duke University Student Jennifer Qi, Majoring in Neuroscience and Anthropology with a Minor in Dance

"For a multi-channel artist, gather the work that means the most to you, that represents you as a person. Each type of art is a different path to express who we truly are. The multitude of expressions and emotions converge to embody us—the people behind the art.

For 14 years, I have been a Chinese dancer, filmmaker, photographer, and musical theater director, so it was very hard for me to organize my work into a common theme. If you're a multi-channel artist like me, I suggest you investigate a larger common ground of your works through the following questions:

A) What do I create art for?

Your initial answer is probably along the lines of "to create a channel between reality and my ideal world." But for your art portfolio, you must be more specific in explaining the themes of your ideal world. For example, mine would be equality, motherhood, cultural identity, storytelling, developing technology, ethics, family, love, etc.

B) Do I have a certain style? If so, what is it?

Every artist has their own style, whether it is surrealist, classicist, impressionist, pop, regional, conceptual, etc., and sometimes even a fusion. Defining your own style of art not only provides you with more insight into how to design your portfolio, but also serves as a chance to know yourself and your creations through a different angle.

C) How can I manifest my uniqueness among other genius artists?

This is the most important question to consider because the diversity in art means no 2 styles are comparable. Remember that your identity as a multi-channel artist is already a "value add" for your chosen school. There are two ways to manifest uniqueness in this case: 1) consider something representative of you and 2) consider something representative for the admission officer.

When I was applying to college, I choreographed a Chinese ethnic dance that stood for a red dragonfly, a myth from a Yi minority group. That represented my uniqueness as an applicant since an outsider cannot easily grasp the spiritual essence of a Chinese ethnic group from just one performance. Additionally, I included my experience of directing 3 renowned Broadway musicals—*Dear Evan Hansen* (2021), *Hamilton* (2022), *In The Heights* (2023)—in my portfolio. By contrast, those were experiences that any college admissions officer would recognize and understand at once how impressive they were."

Final Thoughts on Your Portfolio

Be yourself! Let your portfolio represent who you are by reflecting your strengths, interests, and experiences.

Aim for artwork that is new, fresh, and about something that matters to you.

"We review the visual art application portfolios via online portals, where everything can be altered digitally to appear 'perfect.' And while clarity and conscientiousness is fundamental to the application process, applicants who embrace their real-world imperfections tend to stand out. My advice to teens applying online is to try and capture the unique quirks of your work, no matter the medium. Let these "imperfections" set you apart and express your unique point of view. Your application (and ultimately, your art practice) should try to answer the question *who are you?* —**Tomas Vu-Daniel, Artistic Director of the LeRoy Neiman Center for Print Studies at Columbia University**

If you share what you are most excited about in your artwork, colleges and universities will have no problem seeing what makes you unique and special.

"Ultimately, it's all about passion and ideas, and so if you include the kinds of things that you're most excited about, that you're most proud of, then chances are your portfolio submission will make a strong impression."—**Ringling College of Art and Design**

"Neither a lofty degree of intelligence nor imagination go to the making of genius. Love, love, love, that is the soul of genius."—Wolfgang Amadeus Mozart

Colleges are not looking for perfection—they are looking for a love of learning. Show your heart in your portfolio.

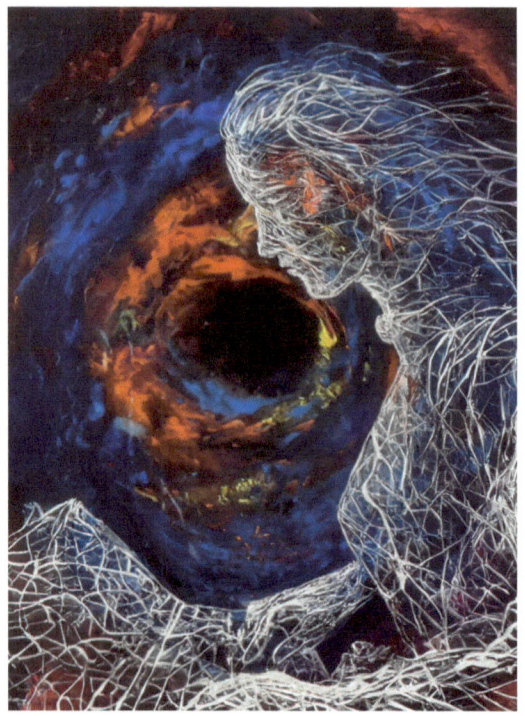

Artwork courtesy of Amy Shi, accepted to Rice University majoring in Biosciences

Title: Musings in a Void
Medium: Oil paint and Acrylic
Year: 2024

Artwork courtesy of Juhi Kundu, accepted to Princeton
University majoring in Mechanical Engineering

Title: Dying Rose
Material: Acrylic paint
Year: 2024

Supplemental 2: How To Write an Artist Statement for College

"An artist statement is a piece of writing by you that helps the audience access or understand your artistic work. It is written in the first person."—**School of the Art Institute of Chicago (SAIC)**

T he artist statement is a description of your artistic style, the type of art you create, and the reasons why. Be specific by using examples. This is an opportunity to show your academic side but still use creative and descriptive language to explain your concepts, ideas, and process. Fill at least half a page and up to one full page to communicate your technical skills and explain what inspires you.

"One way to write in your true voice is to record yourself. Imagine you are telling someone your responses to these questions: Why am I an artist? Why do I do my art? Why do I feel this way about art? Talk about your first memory doing your art or about who inspires you and why."
—University of North Carolina School of the Arts

"Your statement is for explaining why you're driven to make it: What drives you to be an artist? What will keep you going through art school? Who or what are your influences as an artist?"
—**California College of the Arts (CCA)**

Include some of the following points:

- Why you created the artwork
- Your overall vision
- Sources and inspiration for your images
- Artists you have been influenced by or how your work relates to that of other artists
- Other influences
- How your artwork fits into a series or larger body of work
- How a certain technique is important to your work
- Your philosophy about making art

The final paragraph should summarize the most important points in the statement.

As you apply to various institutions, you may want to tweak your statement to best match the particular school or its requirements. Highlight your skills and goals to match with those of the college (read the school's motto, vision statement, and values to help you articulate why you are a good match).

"A well-written artist statement will provide background information to enhance a viewer's appreciation of your artwork. Information can include but is not limited to origin, process, artistic influences, or purpose."—**Rhode Island School of Design (RISD)**

Questions to ask yourself:

- What am I trying to say in my artwork?
- What influences my work?
- How do my methods of working (techniques, style, decisions) support the content of my work?
- What are specific examples of this in my work?

"Focus on the things that matter most to you such as color, mark, composition, materials, concept, and process."—**Rhode Island School of Design (RISD)**

Writing style tips:

- Be genuine.
- Try to capture your own speaking voice.
- Avoid repetition of phrases and words.
- Vary sentence structure and length. The length of a sentence should relate to the complexity of the idea.
- Organization of detail is important. Significant ideas should be at the end of each sentence for emphasis.

"We want to hear your story. What inspires you? What are you interested in?"
—University of the Arts, London (UAL)

If you show genuine enthusiasm for art, colleges will have no problem seeing what makes you unique and special.

"Be yourself. Everyone else is already taken."
—Oscar Wilde

College admissions teams want to know YOU. Let your personality and curiosity shine through in your artist statement and your work.

Artwork courtesy of Valentine Liu, accepted to The New School, Parsons School of Design

Title: Tea Break
Material: Wood Cut, Oil Ink
Year: 2023

Artwork courtesy of Valentine Liu, accepted to The
New School, Parsons School of Design

Title: House In Tibet
Material: Wood Cut, Oil Ink
Year: 2023

Supplemental 3: Write a Memorable College Essay

College application season can feel overwhelming, especially when it is time to sit down and write your essays. But think of your essays as your chance to speak directly to admissions officers—your voice, your story, your song. If that sounds daunting, don't worry! Here is how to write memorable essays that showcase the best version of yourself.

The Personal Statement: Telling Your Story

Your personal statement is like a single, resonant note that tells admissions officers, *This is who I am.* But what should you write about?

What to Write About:

1. **Find your core topic:** Pick a moment, habit, or something you are interested in that defines who you are. Reflect on the last one or two years—what experiences changed or shaped you?
2. **Keep it narrow:** Don't try to squeeze in your whole life story. Focus on one meaningful event or observation and explore it deeply.

3. **Play your "one song":** What is the one thing you want admissions to remember about you? Show them, through your story, why you are interesting, creative, or driven.

4. **Highlight growth:** Did you overcome an obstacle or discover something new about yourself? Share what you learned, who helped you, and how it changed you and your thinking.

How to Write It:

- **Show, don't tell:** Instead of writing, "I learned perseverance," describe the late nights, a setback, and the moment you pushed through. Bring your reader into the story.

- **Be specific:** Avoid vague statements like "I love art." Instead, talk about how you spent weeks working on a charcoal portrait, focusing on every detail of the subject's eyes, until they finally looked alive on the page.

- **Be enthusiastic:** Your writing voice should sparkle with energy and curiosity. Think of this as your chance to make someone say, "I want this student on my campus!"

The "Why" Essay: Making the Match

This essay answers two big questions:

1. Why do you belong at this college?
2. What will you bring to their community?

What to Write About

- **Personal fit:** Show that you have done your homework about the college. What programs, professors, or opportunities excite you, and why?
- **Your contribution:** How will you enrich campus life? Use examples from your academic, cultural, or co-curricular experiences to illustrate what you will bring.
- **Your goals:** Share what you hope to learn and achieve at this specific college.

Writing Tips

- **Be specific:** Instead of saying, "I admire your art program," mention a professor whose lectures on Renaissance art history inspire you, or a student exhibit you saw that left an impression.
- **Show your creativity:** Let your curiosity and ideas shine through. Share your excitement about techniques, styles, or artistic projects you'd love to tackle.
- **Be genuine:** Admissions officers want to hear your genuine voice, not a list of buzzwords from their website.

Pitfalls to Avoid

Writing about yourself can feel tricky, but steering clear of these common missteps will help:

1. **Too broad or generic:** Avoid clichés or topics everyone writes about, like "cross-cultural awareness" or "hard work." Focus on what makes *you* special. Look to small moments or observations.
2. **Negativity overload:** Even if you have faced struggles, highlight how you have grown. Colleges want to admit students who are resilient and bring positive energy.
3. **Too personal:** Think of your essay like a professional statement of purpose, not a diary entry.
4. **Long introductions:** Jump into your story quickly! Admissions officers do not have time for slow build-ups.

Arts Originated from the Unexpected: Duke University Student Jennifer Qi's Story

"Studying and practicing art has never been a normal or easy thing in the traditional Chinese education system I was raised in. When all the teachers and classmates care about are grades and competition, it was nearly impossible to experience something creative, boundless, and innately human.

After I enrolled at an international high school, my story with arts began. In the rapidly fleeting spring of the 11th grade, I directed a short film, The Birthmark, which was sent to five international film festivals and, unexpectedly, won competitive prizes. I had fulfilled a long-cherished wish. Like the Chinese musician Pu

Shu writes in his song "On The Road," "We passed by happiness, passed by pain, passed through the endless cold and loneliness of life." I had dismantled myself, broke my heart into small pieces, crumbled them up, and offered them to art, to the story.

On a Sunday evening in March, I watched the sunset devour the stainless steel of the overpass inch by inch, disappearing at the edge of the horizon. Thirty slow-motion shots on the camera instantly took up a third of the memory card. I walked back and forth over a few meters of road 31 times. On the overcrowded Route 88 bus, we rode from the west of Beijing to the east and back, just to capture the perfect intensity for the opening shot. The deep purple of dusk melted into the evening, and the mountain peach blossoms of spring were lighter than the wind.

In June, I returned to a familiar, vibrant, and resilient crew for our school's musical. Interactions with people here were always vivid but fleeting. Time slipped away from the makeshift nest built with cushions in the international department's basement and from the knife trying to saw through a raw log on the stage. When the soul loses its temple, rain falls on the heart. A group of peers completed a dream about music together—a dream with no concept of victory or success. The moment at which the finale ended was the beginning.

Musical theater is a magical art form because it transcends debates like "Is art meant to express itself or to resonate with the audience?" Musical theater itself is the change. It boldly connects the hearts of performers and audiences, reaching a scope beyond any other form of performance.

So, if you ask me: Does destination matter? I now feel that where you arrive is no longer important. What matters is starting the journey. Rather than directly obtaining the result, I would leave behind the most vivid pulse, the purest faith. I would enjoy the stubborn, inexplicable process. That is what my work in the arts has taught me."

Final Thoughts: Project Strength and Positivity

The best essays project energy, curiosity, confidence, and show what you will add to the university. Think of your personal statement as the song that introduces *you*, and your "Why" essay as the encore that shows you're ready for college.

Be honest, specific, and excited about your future. Admissions officers will hear your individual story loud and clear—and they'll want to see you on their campus stage.

Now, grab your keyboard and start writing your song!

"Art is not what you see, but what you make others see."—**Edgar Degas**

Your art is important because it helps others feel or see something new. That is what colleges are looking for—your perspective, not just technical skill.

Artwork courtesy of Jack Dylan Zimmerman, accepted to Washington University in St. Louis majoring in Design.

Title: Starboard Abyss
Medium: Oil on canvas
Year: 2024

Artwork courtesy of Jack Dylan Zimmerman, accepted to
Washington University in St. Louis majoring in Design

Title: Isolated Views
Medium: Oil on canvas
Year: 2024

Supplemental 4: Art Terms to Use In Your Standout Portfolio

As you create an art portfolio to supplement your college application, do you wonder how you should describe your art?

Use these art terms in your portfolio descriptions to show off your art knowledge and distinguish yourself academically as well as artistically.

The description of each piece should be about 2–4 sentences packed with information. Admissions committees have thousands of portfolios to review, and they know how to do it *fast*. That means your descriptions need to be succinct and effective. Include the following:

- **Title**
- **Medium(s)**
- **Dimensions**
- **Date created.** All work should be recent, i.e. within the last four years of high school (secondary school).

Also, use the exact names of the colors that come out of the paint tubes to describe your art instead of generic terms like red, blue, yellow, green, etc. See how the following words are more vivid?

Yellow Ochre
Raw Sienna
Burnt Sienna
Cadmium Yellow
Cadmium Red
Crimson
Scarlet
Cobalt Violet
Ultramarine Blue
Cerulean Blue
Manganese Blue Hue
Phthalo Green
Turquoise
Burnt Umber
Gold
Iridescent White
Charcoal Gray
Mars Black
Indigo

In the description of each piece, explain how you created it and why. What do you think was successful? Were there any challenges? What do you want the viewer to take away from experiencing your art?

Pick whatever terms align with your piece to 1) showcase your art knowledge and 2) sound informed and educated on art techniques and art history references. This shows colleges your academic side as well as your creative side.

Art Vocabulary

Allegory: In art, allegory is when the subject of the artwork, or the various elements that form the composition, is used to symbolize a deeper moral or spiritual meaning such as life, death, love, virtue, justice, etc.

Avant-garde: a French phrase that means "vanguard" or "advance guard." In art, it refers to works that are innovative and push boundaries, exploring new forms or subject matter. It can also refer to the artist or movement that created the art. Avant-garde art is often aesthetically innovative, but may initially be unacceptable to the artistic establishment of the time.

Brushwork: In oil painting, brushwork refers to the way an artist applies paint to a canvas using a brush. It can be thick or thin, smooth or rough, and can convey different textures and emotions depending on the artist's intention.

Chiaroscuro: an Italian art term that means "light-dark" and refers to the use of contrasting light and shade in a painting or drawing to create the illusion of volume, mass, and three-dimensionality. It can also be used to emphasize and illuminate important figures, or to create drama or mystery.

Composition: the term given to a complete work of art and, more specifically, to the way in which all its elements work together to produce an overall effect.

Depth: In art, depth is the illusion of three-dimensional space on a two-dimensional surface. It can also refer to the apparent distance between objects in a work of art, or how close or far away they appear.

Diptych: an artwork consisting of two painted or carved panels that form a pair.

Figurative art: art that is representational and clearly derived from real-world sources, such as objects, figures, or scenes. The term is often used in contrast to abstract art and can be applied to a wide range of media, including paintings, sculptures, illustrations, photography, and film.

Focal point: a specific area, element, or spot that draws the viewer's eye and attention. It's usually the most important part of the piece and stands out from the rest of the composition. Focal points can be created using color, light, line, or movement, and they can also be outside of the artwork.

Foreground: the part of a composition that is closest to the viewer, or appears to be. It is usually located in the lower part of the picture, immediately behind the picture plane.

Genre: a type or category of painting, such as Renaissance, Rococo, Impressionism, Abstract Expressionism, or Pop Art. A genre can also refer to the content or topic of a particular picture, such as a scene of everyday life.

Genre art can depict ordinary people and their activities, such as markets, domestic settings, interiors, parties, inn scenes, work, and street scenes. These representations can be realistic, imagined, or romanticized by the artist.

A genre can also encompass artworks that share the same criteria, principles, or methods. This can be applied to all art forms, including painting, sculpture, film, and literature.

Glazing: a technique that has been used by artists for centuries to create luminous, glowing effects in their works. It involves applying thin, translucent layers of paint over a dried base layer of paint, building up layers of glaze to create depth and complexity.

Harmony: the visually satisfying effect of combining similar, related elements, e.g. adjacent colors on the color wheel, similar shapes, etc.

Landscape: a type of artwork that depicts natural scenery as its main subject. Also known as landscape painting, it can include mountains, forests, rivers, valleys, trees, and bodies of water. Landscape art can also include man-made structures and people, and often features a wide view with a coherent composition. The sky is almost always included, and weather is sometimes an element of the composition.

The term "landscape" comes from the Dutch *landschap*, which originally meant "region" or "tract of land". In the early 16th century, it took on an artistic connotation to mean "a picture depicting scenery on land." The history of landscape painting can be traced back to ancient times, when the Greeks and Romans created wall paintings of landscapes and gardenscapes. However, until the 17th century, landscapes were often relegated to the background of paintings and portraits that focused on religious, mythological, or historical subjects.

Landscape art can take many forms, including drawings, paintings, sculptures, or etchings. It can be realistic, abstract, or surreal, and artists can take creative liberties to rearrange elements in a scene to create a compelling composition. Landscape art can also convey the artist's emotions and appreciation for nature, and can have religious significance or evolve into a means of self-expression.

Line: Line art or line drawing is any image that consists of distinct straight lines or curves placed against a background (usually plain), without gradations in shade (darkness) or hue (color) to represent two-dimensional or three-dimensional objects.

Mixed media: In visual art, mixed media describes artwork in which more than one medium or material has been employed. Assemblages, collages, and sculpture are three common examples of art using different media. Materials used to create mixed media art include, but are not limited to, paint, cloth, paper, wood, and found objects.

Motif: a recurring fragment, theme, or pattern that appears in a work of art.

Narrative: simply a story. Narrative art is art that tells a story. Much of Western art until the 20th century has been narrative, depicting stories from religion, myth and legend, history, and literature.

Perspective: a technique that uses mathematical principles to create the illusion of depth and distance on a two-dimensional surface, such as a canvas, by representing three-dimensional objects. Artists can use perspective to create realistic images, or to create dramatic or disorienting effects.

Proportion: refers to the dimensions of a composition and relationships between height, width, and depth. How proportion is used will affect how realistic or stylized something seems. Proportion also describes how the sizes of different parts of a piece of art or design relate to each other.

Scale: the overall physical size of an artwork or objects in the artwork. We always relate scale to the size of the human body—how big or small the piece is in relation to us. An artist may decide to use a scale which is different from life-sized, and this will have an impact on how it feels.

Symbolism: an aesthetic movement that uses symbols and motifs to represent ideas and subjects, and to create underlying meaning. Symbolist artists reject the realistic depiction of the natural world in favor of imaginary dream worlds, and believe that art should reflect emotions and ideas rather than represent the natural world. Their work often includes mysterious figures from literature, mythology, and the Bible, and common themes include love, fear, death, and personal awakening. Symbolist art can also be dreamlike, surreal, and fantastical, and may explore the human psyche, dreams, fantasies, and the unconscious mind.

The term "symbolism" was coined in 1886 by French critic Jean Moréas to describe the poetry of Stéphane Mallarmé and Paul Verlaine, and soon spread to visual art throughout Europe. Some notable Symbolist painters include Odilon Redon, Edvard Munch, Paul Gauguin, Gustave Moreau, and Gustav Klimt.

Texture: the perceived surface quality of a work of art. It may be perceived physically (through the sense of touch), or visually, or both. Our experience of texture in visual art relies on our experience with the physical world.

Theme: a broad idea or a message conveyed by a work, such as a performance, a painting, a motion picture, or a video game. This message is usually about life, society, or human nature.

Triptych: an artwork, usually a painting or photograph, formed as a trio. Originating in the Middle Ages, the art form was intended to be displayed together and consisted of a substantial center with two adjoining smaller wings, which could be folded to protect the panels.

Value: Rather than indicating the monetary worth of fine art on the art market, the value of art refers to the lightness or darkness of a color. Every color has a value between white and black, and every shade can be arranged on a gradient value scale.

Sometimes liberal arts colleges will send the portfolio to the visual art faculty to review, so incorporate a few of these art terms into the descriptions in your portfolio to show your art knowledge and expertise. Refer to famous artist influences or art movements throughout history, and college admission readers will be impressed!

Remember to include in the description what you created and how (colleges like to know about your thinking and making process, and how a work of art developed). Most importantly, reflect on why you created it and how it fits into your overall artistic theme.

"Don't only practice your art, but force your way into its secrets."—**Ludwig van Beethoven**

Dig deep. Learn everything you can. Push yourself to understand your craft—because that is how you grow as an artist and as a person.

Artwork courtesy of Yuki Sun, accepted to Sarah Lawrence
College majoring in Film Directing and Playwriting

Title: Justice
Medium: Procreate digital art
Year: 2021

99

Artwork courtesy of Yuki Sun, accepted to Sarah Lawrence College majoring in Film Directing & Playwriting

Title: The Star
Material: Digital Art
Year: 2020

Supplemental 5: How to Talk About Art

E ven with the right vocabulary, talking about art can be challenging. You might look at a painting or sculpture and think, *What do I even say about this?* Relax—you don't have to be an expert to talk about art. Whether you're in a visual arts class, at a museum, or just chatting with friends, having a few key terms in your back pocket can help you sound knowledgeable.

Let's break it down together!

Balance

When we talk about *balance* in art, we are looking at how elements are arranged in a piece. Think of it like a scale—if too much is happening on one side, it can feel off.

Artists use balance to create harmony. It can be symmetrical (both sides look the same) or asymmetrical (both sides are different but still feel balanced). Next time you look at a painting or sculpture, ask yourself, *Does this feel balanced?*

Contrast

Contrast is about opposites. Light and dark, rough and smooth, big and small—when artists use contrast, they are trying to make things stand out. It grabs your attention and adds drama.

When you are describing art, think about where the artist used contrast and how it makes you feel. Does it make the artwork more intense? More exciting? More interesting?

Scale and Proportion

These two terms are all about size and how things relate to each other.

Scale refers to the size of an object in relation to something else—like a huge statue in a park or a tiny figurine in a big room.

Proportion is about the relationship between the sizes of different parts of an object or figure. Is the head bigger than the body? Or is everything in perfect proportion?

These details can change how we see and feel about the art.

Rhythm

You might think rhythm only applies to music, but it is used in art too! *Rhythm* in visual art refers to the repetition of shapes, colors, or lines. It creates a sense of movement, like your eyes are dancing across the canvas. Rhythm adds energy and life to the work.

When you are talking about rhythm in art, think about how your eyes move around the piece. Is there a flow? A beat?

Why These Terms Matter

Using these terms isn't just about sounding smart—they give you a way to *connect* with the art. When you describe what you are seeing and feeling, the whole experience becomes richer. Art isn't just about looking; it is about thinking, feeling, and understanding. And when you have the language to express how you are experiencing a piece of art, you get much more out of it.

Art is for Enjoyment

At the end of the day, art is meant to be enjoyed. It is a way to contemplate life, express yourself, and feel something. There is no right or wrong way to talk about it—just your way. Use these terms as a tool to explore and share your thoughts, but remember to have fun with the art.

So next time you are in front of a painting or sculpture, give it a try. Look for balance, contrast, scale, proportion, and rhythm. And don't be afraid to share your thoughts! I hope you enjoy the experience of art as much as I do.

"Everyone discusses my art and pretends to understand, as if it were necessary to understand, when it is simply necessary to love."—**Claude Monet**

Not everyone will "get" your work, and that is okay. One way to share it is with love and let others respond in their own way. (But explanations will be part of art school dialogues!)

Artwork courtesy of Victor Fu-Zhou, college applicant, Interlake
High School, WA

Title: Curiosity
Medium: Photography
Year: 2025

Artwork courtesy of Sisi Zhang, college applicant, The Stony Brook School, NY

Title: Moment
Medium: Photography
Year: 2025

Supplemental 6: Wabi-Sabi: Finding Beauty in Imperfection

A message for teen artists preparing their college portfolios

I first heard the term *wabi-sabi* in a yoga class a few years ago. We were swaying in and out of a balancing pose when the teacher quietly said, "Let it be *wabi-sabi*." I didn't know then what the term meant, but I felt my body relax.

Later I learned that *wabi-sabi* is a Japanese philosophy centered around imperfection, impermanence, and simplicity. It is the art of noticing what is quiet and real, even flawed, and seeing it as beautiful.

There is also a related practice called *kintsugi*, the Japanese art of mending broken pottery with golden or silver seams. Instead of hiding the cracks, kintsugi makes them shimmer. The gold-lined fractures become part of the story. They symbolize repair and healing. They remind us that this object has a purpose. It has broken and been made whole again. That wholeness can be considered even more beautiful for its history.

As teen artists creating portfolios, imperfection is meaningful. You are not presenting a flawless version of yourself; rather, you are showing who you are *becoming*.

Your Portfolio Is Not About Perfection

Some of the most memorable student art I have seen is rooted in the spirit of *wabi-sabi*, even if the artist didn't consider the term when making it.

A black and white photograph of a child reaching toward shiny objects in a shop window. The child's face is soft with wonder. The reflection is smudged. The composition is delicate and luminous.

A close-up of the inside of a flower, abstracted until it resembles a petri dish of vibrant life, like a secret ecosystem unfolding in plain sight.

A sculptural black ring positioned in a Seattle park, its circular void perfectly framing the Space Needle in the distance. Minimal yet intentional, and all about alignment.

A quiet trip to a seashore park, captured in documentary images. The artist expected to find nothing special... until they stumbled across a driftwood shelter. It was pieced together by someone unknown. The structure stood weathered and handmade against a backdrop of rocks and sky.

I think of a photograph a student once shared with me that showed drops of condensation on a dorm room air conditioner. The droplets blurred the view outside, turning an ordinary moment into something meditative that looked like pouring rain.

Another student took a photograph from the back of a church bus at dusk. Everyone else had fallen asleep. Inside, the bus was dark. Outside, a pale sunset cast a soft glow on the edge of the world. These images are not complex, but they are alive with emotion and timing.

There was another photo that caught my eye of a deer foraging near a school dormitory, its rough brown coat blending into the crackle of dry leaves. The textures were earthy, nothing special, just a simple encounter.

These moments hold stillness and space. They draw us into the kind of seeing that takes time, care, and presence. They are not overly refined.

Seeing with a Wabi-Sabi Lens

In some Western art traditions, the expectation is to arrive at a finished product that looks impressive. But *wabi-sabi* invites us into a different rhythm that values subtlety.

This shift in perspective helps us:

- **Reframe failure.** Cracks are not flaws to hide. They are signs of experience. Like gold in the pottery seams, your mistakes and missteps can be reframed as part of your development and learning.
- **Practice self-acceptance.** You do not have to prove that you are perfect. You can share work that is emotional and evolving.
- **See yourself as capable.** The work you have done so far already carries weight. Your creative instincts, experiments, and observations are evidence of who you are becoming.

Let Your Portfolio Breathe

Don't be afraid to include pieces that feel in-progress, minimal, or imperfect. Let your portfolio be a story of growth. Leave space for the viewer to feel something, and invite them to slow down.

Remember the child reaching in the window. The hidden world inside a flower. The driftwood shelter on the shore.

These are not polished masterpieces, but poems made from attention.

A Different Way of Seeing

In many Western art traditions, there is a tendency to aim for the big moment. The masterpiece is praised for its technique. But Eastern philosophies, like those that shaped *wabi-sabi*, value simplicity and space. An ink painting might feature more blank paper than brushstroke. A piece of ceramic might be prized for its irregularity.

Learning to recognize both approaches will help you grow in your art practice. Remember that there are many ways to be an artist, and different ways to see.

Artwork courtesy of Jack Dylan Zimmerman, accepted to
Washington University in St. Louis (WashU) majoring in Design

Title: Clouded Minds
Medium: Charcoal and watercolor on paper
Year: 2024

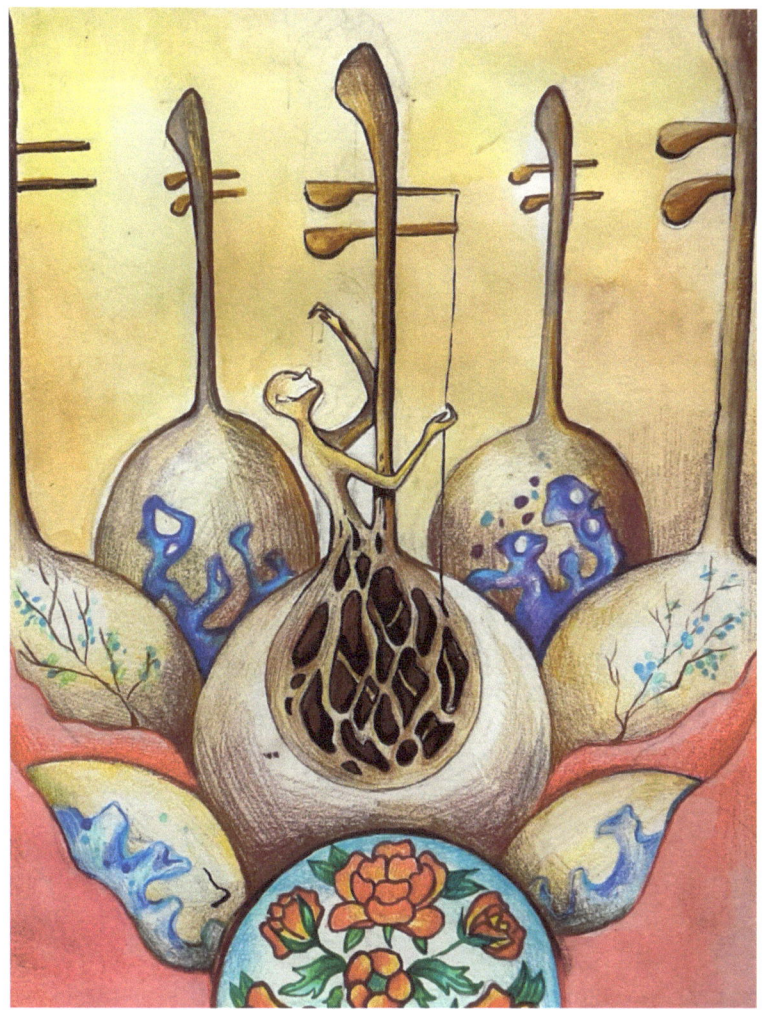

Artwork courtesy of Jean Kwak, accepted to Chelsea College of Art, University of the Arts London

Title: Haegeum (Korean musical instrument)
Medium: Colored pencil, watercolour paint on paper
Year: 2021

Supplemental 7: Creative Ways to Reconnect with Your Artistic Self

E ven the most creative people sometimes get stuck. Whether you are a photographer, a painter, a writer, or a dancer, the artistic rut is real. We start to question ourself, compare our work to others, and wonder if what we are doing matters. But here is the truth: doubt and comparison are part of the creative path. The key is learning how to move through them with curiosity rather than fear.

One of my students, a thoughtful Comparative Literature and Photography major, recently found herself in a low place creatively. She felt uninspired and stuck, unsure of how to reconnect with her vision. Then, she did something powerful—she acknowledged what she was feeling. That kind of self-awareness is the first and most important step.

Then, she took action. She switched cameras, not because one was better than the other, but because she wanted to *see differently*. A change in tools can lead to a change in mindset. After that, she began photographing familiar things—her dorm room, her daily life. These were not glamorous shots meant to impress. They were intimate moments: her lamp, her desk, the light through her window. They were exercises in seeing.

And then something beautiful happened.

She began layering calligraphy over her photographs, adding poetry, quotes from famous works of literature, and personal thoughts right on top of the images. What once felt mundane became expressive, layered, and rich with meaning. "Instead of noticing the most impressive and gorgeous," she told me, "I pay close attention to my daily life."

Her portfolio now centers on home, the sky, self-reflection, and the story behind the ordinary. It is genuine and connects to her narrative.

If you are feeling stuck, try one of these ideas to help shake off doubt and reconnect with your creative self:

1. Switch Up Your Tools
Try a different camera, brush, journal, or digital tool. A new texture or lens can refresh the way you see the world.

2. Document the Ordinary
Photograph or draw what is around you—your kitchen table, your shoes by the door, the afternoon light. These small details carry so much story.

3. Add a New Layer
Combine disciplines. Add handwritten notes, sketches, or found objects to your work. Let yourself experiment. Playfulness is a cure for perfectionism.

4. Change the Format
Print your photos on large matte paper with a ragged edge for a handmade feel. Or publish them in a small book format with titles or stories. It's not about the final product—it is about seeing your work in a new way.

5. Curate Your Own Mini Gallery
Put your work up on your wall. Move it around. See how one piece feels next to another. This act of arranging can reveal unexpected connections between your ideas.

6. Share Your Creations
Share a small book of your work with friends or family. Not for feedback—just for connection. Art doesn't always need a grade; sometimes it just needs to be seen.

If you are in a rut, it doesn't mean you have failed. It means you are being invited to slow down, look closer, and rediscover why you started creating in the first place. Believe me, your pace will soon increase with the excitement in something new, a clever development, connection, or approach.

You don't need to be the most impressive or the most original. You are genuine just the way you are. And sometimes, the most powerful art comes from the most overlooked corners of our daily lives.

Artwork courtesy of Shayna Shapiro, accepted to the Fashion Institute of Technology (FIT) with a major in Advertising and Marketing Communications

Untitled
Medium: Photography
Year: 2020

Artwork courtesy of Shayna Shapiro, accepted to the Fashion Institute of Technology (FIT) with a major in Advertising and Marketing Communications

Untitled
Medium: Photography
Year: 2020

Supplemental 8: The Value of an Arts Degree

W hy is it valuable to earn a degree in the arts?

An art degree will develop your skills in:

1) **Creativity and innovation**—By encouraging you to think outside the box and solve problems with original ideas.

2) **Collaboration**—Working alongside peers on group projects and critiques.

3) **Self-discipline**—Through the dedication required to meet deadlines and continuously refine your craft.

4) **Flexibility**—Taking a variety of art courses prepares you to be flexible in your future career.

5) **Research**—The research-intensive nature of arts programs also molds students with strong analytical and critical-thinking skills.

What is the value of a music degree?

A music degree will teach you to:

1) Give (and take) constructive criticism.
2) Receive guidance from industry professionals, such as museum curators, award-winning writers, and renowned artists. Often, these professionals have a residency or are part of the school faculty. This career guidance can aid in seeking and obtaining internships or jobs.
3) Develop emotional intelligence by empathizing with the composer and audience.
4) Bring your ideas and visions to life.

More to love about an arts degree:

1) The arts often foster a close-knit community and smaller class size. This means students are more engaged and receive personalized attention.
2) Higher education helps teens transition into adults, and arts education is known for fostering critical thinking, analytical skills, and the ability to interpret complex information.
3) Studies show these skills are transferable to various professional fields, along with adaptability and flexibility gained from an interdisciplinary learning environment.

4) A master's degree can enhance your portfolio, increase networking opportunities, advance your art career, or prepare you for college-level teaching.

Careers supported by a music degree:

1) Many graduates are self-employed and work as freelancers.
2) The music industry—sharing your musical talents with others.
3) Music technology—marketing, media, and communication.
4) Arts administration—directing a museum or non-profit arts organization.
5) Music therapy—helping people to heal through music.
6) Music education—teaching your musical skills to children, teens, or adults.

College auditions take place from November to February. Many conservatories have December 1 college application deadlines. Prepare your music audition during the summer/fall before senior year (Grade 12 in the U.S.) to feel confident.

Music is not only a pleasant soundtrack, but it can also be the key to the additional resources of our brains, which help us cope with challenges. Did you know?

1) Albert Einstein said that whenever he was stuck on a scientific problem, he would take a break to clear his mind by playing his beloved violin.
2) Fictional detective Sherlock Holmes improvised on the violin to enable him to figure out equations and problems.

"An artist's duty is to reflect the times in which we live."—**Nina Simone**

Think about how your work connects to the world. Even small choices in your art can say something powerful about your community, culture, or generation.

Artwork courtesy of Jean Kwak, accepted to Chelsea College of Art, University of the Arts London

Title: Melody in the night
Medium: Colored pencil, colour conte on black paper
Year: 2021

Artwork courtesy of Jean Kwak accepted to Chelsea College of Art, University of the Arts London

Title: Portrait of Jacob Collier (musician)
Medium: Poster colour, watercolor paint, colored pencil on paper
Year: 2022

Supplemental 7: Crafting an Impressive Video Introduction for a College Music Application

P reparing a video introduction for a prestigious college like University of Southern California (USC) can feel daunting, but with the right approach, you can create something that feels personal and polished, and that powerfully showcases your enthusiasm for music. Whether you play the violin, flute, saxophone, or any other instrument, here's a step-by-step guide to help you shine on camera.

1. Speak Naturally
Think of your video as a casual conversation with a friend or family member. While it is good to prepare what you will say, avoid reading directly from a script. Instead, jot down key points on a card and place it off camera so you can glance at it for guidance. This way, your delivery will feel genuine and relatable. Practice a few times until you are comfortable speaking in your natural voice.

2. Start with a Strong Introduction
Begin by establishing a personal connection by sharing your name, high school, and hometown. Here is an example: "Hi, I'm Anna Mason, a senior at Lakeside High School in Atlanta, Georgia. Music has been my interest for as long as I

can remember, and I'm excited to share a little about myself and why I'm applying to USC."

3. Share Your Musical Development
After introducing yourself, tell your story. Include:

- The instrument you play and how you got started with it.
- What excites you about music.
- Your favorite songs or musicians and how they have influenced you.
- Any outstanding performances or programs you have participated in as well as any awards you've received.

For example, a flutist might say: "I've been playing the flute since I was eight years old. From the moment I held the instrument, its shiny beauty captivated me. I've always been inspired by flutist Marina Piccinini—her artistry and enthusiasm for pushing the boundaries of what the flute can do are incredible. Watching her perform opened my eyes to how dynamic and expressive the flute can be, and it made me want to find my own voice through music."

"One of my proudest moments was performing as a soloist at the state honor band festival last year. I also had the incredible opportunity to play in a summer program at [program name], where I worked with top-notch musicians and even performed a duet at the final concert. When I think back on those experiences, I'm reminded of why I love music and how they have fueled my desire to keep growing as a performer."

4. Tie Your Interest to USC

Make a strong connection between your interests and what USC offers. Research their programs, faculty, or unique opportunities and explain why they resonate with you.

For instance, you could say: "What excites me most about USC is its commitment to celebrating diverse voices in music. The course on women composers, for example, aligns perfectly with my goal of bringing more visibility to underrepresented artists. I'd love to work with professors like [insert name] to explore how music can tell stories that inspire change."

5. Share Your Vision

Talk about your future aspirations and the impact you want to make through music. Be bold and enthusiastic!

Some ideas are: "I hope to create a platform where young musicians, especially girls, can discover and perform music by female composers. I believe showcasing these works can inspire a new generation to push beyond traditional boundaries and celebrate creativity in all its forms."

6. End with Enthusiasm

Wrap up with gratitude and excitement with something like this: "Thank you for considering my application. I can't wait to bring my enthusiasm for music to the vibrant USC community, and I'm excited about the chance to grow as a musician and as a student."

7. Look the Part

Your appearance should be classy and polished while still reflecting your personality. A clean, stylish outfit in a color or pattern you love can help you feel confident and put together. Your overall look doesn't have to be formal, but it should show that you are serious about this opportunity while letting your individuality shine.

8. Technical Tips

- **Lighting**: Record during the day, facing a window for natural light.
- **Background**: Keep it simple but tidy—a plain wall, bookshelf, or music-related backdrop works great.
- **Sound**: Choose a quiet space and make sure your instrument (if played) is clearly audible.

By following these steps, your video will not only highlight your musical talent but also convey the authenticity and enthusiasm that make you a creative candidate. So take a deep breath, be yourself, and let your interest in music—and your personality—shine!

"The most personal is the most creative."—**Martin Scorsese**

Your unique story is your strength. Share what matters to you, even if it feels small or ordinary. That is what makes it original.

Artwork courtesy of Lia Lee, accepted to Hongik University in Korea majoring in Fashion Design

Title: The Duchess
Medium: Acrylic paints
Year: 2021

Artwork courtesy of Lia Lee, accepted to Hongik University in Korea majoring in Fashion Design

Title: The Favorite
Medium: Acrylic paints
Year: 2021

Afterword

As a college adviser for creative students, I work with thoughtful, talented teens navigating one of the most transformative periods of their lives. While each student's path is different, I have noticed a few constants in how I support them, guide their process, and foster their internal motivation.

Meeting Students Where They Are

Most students who come to me already have family support and a clear direction in the arts. Others have multiple interests—neuroscience, applied math, health, and more—and want to find ways to honor their creativity through photography, visual art, or music in the college application process. These students are often deeply curious and motivated, so we rarely hit roadblocks.

Some come with tension between their personal interests and family expectations. A student might love painting, but their parent or sibling encourages a more "practical" path. I have found that with the right guidance, and a clear plan, families often come to see the value of applying as an artist. One former student wrote a memorable personal statement about her parents removing the door to her room during a difficult time in their relationship, much of it tied to her interest in art. Her story ended with healing and understanding—her parents realizing that her well-being mattered more than any career plan they had imagined for her.

Another student I worked with was interested in neuroscience and also played the oboe. When I asked what he was working on outside of class, he hesitated before sharing that he had been creating '90s-style commercial music jingles just for fun—and had even composed a class song for his graduating year. I encouraged him to include those pieces as part of his creative supplement, showcasing both his artistic flair and sense of humor. His personality shone through, and it became a highlight of his application. He is currently majoring in Neuroscience and playing the oboe at the University of Southern California (USC).

Similarly, one student played keyboard in school ensembles and bands and composed original scores using his digital audio workstation (DAW). Inspired by the music in *How to Train Your Dragon*, he dreamed of composing for film. He was also a talented creative writer. Midway through the application process, however, self-doubt crept in. He made a pivot, deciding to apply as a creative writing major instead of music production. Ultimately, though he was accepted to the University of Miami in Florida, he chose to stay closer to home and attend the University of British Columbia (UBC) in Vancouver, Canada. His story was winding, but real, and I was there to support him and his family with information, a clear plan, and emotional steadiness along the way.

Another student came to me with a laundry list of extracurriculars in her personal statement but no clear message. As I got to know her, I discovered her love for tap dancing and drumming—rhythmic expressions that connected her to her Native American heritage. She had also been adopted and was giving back to her cultural tradition through song and movement by teaching younger children. I encouraged her to build her personal statement around these threads—tap, rhythm, identity, and giving back. It became a powerful essay, full of spirit and connection. She is now enrolled at Rollins College in Florida and majoring in Theatre Arts.

Understanding the Whole Student

My students come from a wide range of academic and language backgrounds. Some are strong writers; others are international students, just beginning to learn how to express themselves in English. One student worried about not knowing the "right" words to say, yet she radiated empathy and joy—qualities that are very important in a holistic college application review.

Even students who face academic challenges rarely say "I can't do this." Instead, they leave our meetings saying things like, "Now I know what I need to do." That clarity builds confidence, and confidence fuels progress.

Wellness and Awareness in the Process

Students who have a healthy grasp on the process are often those who find calm in movement and community. Many participate in athletics—not to become nationally ranked, but for the camaraderie, consistency, and mental clarity. One student ran cross country just to clear her mind and focus on the next mile. She is now majoring in International Affairs at George Washington University in Washington, D.C.

Another student loved taking walks through his neighborhood and photographing what he saw along the way. That same student—who also composed jingles and played the oboe—is now at University of Southern California (USC), studying neuroscience and still playing music.

A classical saxophone player I advised found connection through the Chinese dragon boat community. The physical activity and shared culture gave him a sense of belonging. He is now majoring in Music Performance at Vanderbilt University and loving the campus community.

A current student on the sailing team told me that being on the water brings her peace. Another student, a swimmer, is exploring underwater photography and is passionate about environmental protection. He is interested in the intersection of technology and business.

Other students find balance through their love of nature. One told me how much she looks forward to visiting her aunt's rose garden and simply being among the flowers. She also enjoys packing a picnic with friends, listening closely to their problems, and thinking of ways she can help. These quiet acts of care and reflection create space for clarity.

Some students find relaxation with animals. A few decompress by playing with or snuggling their pet after school. One student found great comfort and purpose volunteering for her school's Paws and Claws Club, where she helped make toys for shelter animals. These simple, tactile moments of kindness—whether with people, pets, or plants—can offer grounding.

And sometimes, wellness looks like giving yourself permission to rest. One student I remember used to sleep the entire ride home on the school bus. The friendly bus driver would wake her up at her stop! Then she would go inside and nap again until dinnertime. Only after she had gotten the rest and nourishment her body needed would she begin her homework. That rhythm worked for her. Listening to your body and trusting your pace works too.

These students have found ways to go to a calm place in their minds—a key skill during the high-pressure college application season.

When students struggle, it is often because they try to skip important steps. Some want to apply early before they have even graduated or completed all their coursework. Others resist taking four full years of core subjects like Mathematics and English. Some limit their college choices too narrowly, only to scramble later when their friends are already set. Others underestimate the workload— supplements, recordings, interviews, and more—on top of keeping up grades and test preparation.[1]

---

[1] Regarding standardized testing information, visit my website where I have written an article, updated regularly, on this topic.

It may sound basic, but staying healthy matters: nutritious food, adequate rest, and a couple of reliable friends to talk with can make all the difference. Students who maintain those habits tend to navigate the process with more resilience and perspective.

Small Touches That Make a Big Difference

My work extends beyond editing essays and researching colleges. I help students define their goals, connect them with alumni, share examples of past portfolios and applications, and keep them on track with regular check-ins—even if it is a news article related to their field or a podcast I think they will enjoy.

For students who are struggling to engage, I offer gentle nudges: short voice memos, encouraging messages, even a meme or two to lighten the mood. Some just need to know they are not alone and that someone cares about their art. And when the creative spark returns—when they finish a music recording, complete an artist statement, or design their creative resume—that is when excitement shows up.

Tools That Work

The most effective tools I have found are not long essays or heavy reading assignments. They are quick, accessible resources: one-minute audio clips, five-minute videos, visual guides or collages that speak volumes with just a few pictures. These formats meet students where they are—in the moment—and make information feel manageable and actionable.

Understanding and Growth

Teen life is full of ups and downs. I do not expect students to be "on" all the time. Instead, I focus on being a consistent presence: a guide who sets expectations, encourages students to reach their potential, and allows room for life to happen along the way.

In the end, I'm a college counselor and art portfolio adviser, but also a creative partner and steady guide. It is fulfilling to watch students shift from unsure to confident and inspired—that is the heart of why I am a college counselor.

In these pages, I have shared a guide to college admissions for teen artists—filled with inspiration, encouragement, and practical tips. My hope is that you now feel confident and equipped to create a standout portfolio that reflects your story.

Remember, college is just the next lily pad on your creative path. You have a lifetime ahead to explore, grow, and offer your gifts to the world through your art.

I wish you all the best as you move forward. If you would like personalized support as you shape your portfolio and college application, I am ready to help. You are also invited to join my creative community at www.danazullo.com where you will find guidance and encouragement.

Keep creating, and stay true to your vision.

Dana Z.

Afterword

Artwork courtesy of Jean Kwak accepted to Chelsea College of
Art, University of the Arts London

Title: Stage
Medium: Colored pencil
Year: 2022

Artwork courtesy of Juhi Kundu, accepted to Princeton University majoring in Mechanical Engineering

Title: Winter Dandelion
Material: Digital Art in Procreate
Year: 2024

Dana's students have been accepted into top institutions with over 1 million dollars in scholarships!

Arizona State University
Art Center College of Design (ACCD)
Berklee College of Music
Boston University
Brown University
California College of the Arts (CCA)
California Institute of the Arts (CalArts)
Chapman University
Chelsea College of Art, University of the Arts London
Cincinnati University
Columbia University
Cornell University
Duke University
Emory University
Fashion Institute of Technology (FIT)
George Washington University (GW)
Washington and Lee University
Georgia Institute of Technology (GT)
Hongik University, Korea
Illinois University
Indiana University
Loyola Marymount University (LMU)
Manhattan School of Music (MSM)
Maryland Institute College of Art (MICA)
New York University (NYU)
North Carolina State University
Oberlin Conservatory of Music
Occidental College
Otis College of Art and Design

The Pennsylvania State University (Penn State)
Pratt Institute
Princeton University
Rhode Island School of Design (RISD)
Rice University
Rollins College
Rutgers University
Sarah Lawrence College
Savannah College of Art and Design (SCAD)
Stanford University (Summer Humanities Institute)
School of the Art Institute of Chicago (SAIC)
School of Visual Arts (SVA)
The New School, Parsons School of Design
University of British Columbia
University of California, Berkeley
University of California, Davis
University of California, Irvine
University of California, Santa Cruz
University of California, San Diego
University of California, Santa Barbara
University of Chicago (pre-college film program)
University of Georgia (UGA)
University of Minnesota
University of San Francisco,
University of Southern California (USC)
University of Sydney, Australia
University of Toronto, Canada
Vanderbilt University
Washington University in St. Louis (WashU)
Yale University
among others

Contributing Artists:

Shayan Ali, University of California San Diego (UCSD)

Victor Fu-Zhou, College applicant

Juhi Kundu, Princeton University

Jean Kwak, Chelsea College of Art, University of the Arts London

Lia Lee, Hongik University, Korea

Valentine Liu, The New School, Parsons School of Design

Amy Pan, Brown University & Rhode Island School of Design

Shayna Shapiro, Fashion Institute of Technology (FIT)

Amy Shi, Rice University

Evan Sun, Emory University

Yuki Sun, Stanford University Pre-College Program & Sarah Lawrence College

Jason Tan, Art Center College of Design (ACCD)

Sisi Zhang, College applicant

Jack Dylan Zimmerman, Washington University in St. Louis (WashU)

Contributions of Advice from College Students:

Lily Gui, Boston University, majoring in Film

Jane, George Washington University, majoring in International Affairs

University of Southern California (USC) student majoring in Neuroscience and oboe player

Jason Tan, Art Center College of Design (ACCD) majoring in Illustration and Entertainment Design

Jennifer Qi, Duke University majoring in Neuroscience and Anthropology with a minor in Dance

Taylor Yi, Vanderbilt University majoring in Music Performance (Classical Saxophone)

Yining Zhang, Washington University in St. Louis (WashU) majoring in Psychology

Dlency Zheng, University of California Los Angeles (UCLA) majoring in Music Industry and Economics

Acknowledgements:

To all of my students—thank you. Your generosity in sharing your artwork, experiences, and advice for younger artists applying to college helped bring this book to life. Your individuality, layered interests, and genuine styles are what make this collection rich and real.

A special thanks to Jason Tan and Lia Lee whose original illustrations and designs for the front and back cover captured the spirit of the book with their energy.

It's been my privilege to advise such talented and creative students over the years. Your work and growth continue to inspire me and elevate everything I do.

Thank you to my Columbia Professor, Tomas Vu-Daniel, Artistic Director of the LeRoy Neiman Center for Print Studies at Columbia University, for his wise words on creating a portfolio.

Appreciation to fellow Columbia graduate and visual artist, Veru Narula for his inspiring words in the foreword. He aimed for the moon- and got his art there!

Thank you to editor, Jessica Andersen. Your steady support and encouragement carried me to the finish line.

I would also like to thank all my teachers along the way, but especially Ikebana floral art Master, Iwalani Barbazon, for her inspiring lessons in design. Her teachings continue to enrich my artistic practice and the creative guidance I offer students.

Thank you to my family for encouraging my art and writing. With heartfelt gratitude to my husband and children for always being at my side, cheering me on through every chapter—literal and figurative. Your belief in me made this book possible.

About the Author

As an experienced art educator and college counselor, Dana Zullo helps visual art and design students create standout portfolios and navigate the college application process with confidence. Her goal is to inspire students to keep learning and growing along their creative storyline. As a published author of artist biographies, Dana guides students in exploring their distinctive qualities and presenting their portfolios in compelling ways.

Holding a degree in Visual Art from Columbia University, a Master's in Education, and design certificates from Emory University, Dana draws on decades of experience in art and design. She worked in notable museums and galleries, including the New York Transit Museum, Caren Golden Fine Art, and Crown Point Press. Her teaching experience extends across cultures—she taught secondary school art for two years in Ghana as a Peace Corps volunteer and later served as a Senior Enrollment Representative at the Savannah College of Art and Design.

She was awarded artist residencies at South Porch Artists in South Carolina, The Writers' Colony at Dairy Hollow in Arkansas, and Sundress Academy for the Arts in Tennessee, where she focused on her poetry. Dana also practices floral art with the Ichiyo School of Ikebana, bringing nature and creativity into everyday spaces.

Dana guides with encouragement, and is dedicated to helping students achieve their goals. She is proud to be the bridge between their aspirations and the opportunities that await them in the arts.

Dana lives in Atlanta, Georgia with her family, and spends part of each summer at Jekyll Island, gathering new inspiration from the sea.

www.danazullo.com

Notes

Notes

Notes

Notes

Notes

Notes